BLESSED NAMES

Why Was He Named Husain (A)?

Written by:
Kisa Kids Publications

Please recite a Fātiḥah for the marḥūmīn
of the Rangwala family, the sponsors of this book.

All proceeds from the sale of this book
will be used to produce more educational resources.

Dedication

This book is dedicated to the beloved Imām of our time (AJ). May Allāh (swt) hasten his reappearance and help us become his true companions.

Acknowledgements

Prophet Muḥammad (s): The pen of a writer is mightier than the blood of a martyr.

True reward lies with Allāh, but we would like to sincerely thank Shaykh Salim Yusufali and Sisters Sabika Mitha Liliana Villalvazo, Zahra Sabur, Kisae Nazar, Sarah Assaf, Nadia Dossani, Fatima Hussain, Naseem Rangwala, a Zehra Abbas. We would especially like to thank Nainava Publications for their contributions. May Allāh bless them this world and the next.

Preface

Prophet Muḥammad (s): Nurture and raise your children in the best way. Raise them with the love of the Proph and the Ahl al-Bayt (a).

Literature is an influential form of media that often shapes the thoughts and views of an entire generation. Therefo in order to establish an Islamic foundation for the future generations, there is a dire need for compelling Islar literature. Over the past several years, this need has become increasingly prevalent throughout Islamic centers a schools everywhere. Due to the growing dissonance between parents, children, society, and the teachings of Isl and the Ahl al-Bayt (a), this need has become even more pressing. Al-Kisa Foundation, along with its subsidia Kisa Kids Publications, was conceived in an effort to help bridge this gap with the guidance of *ʿulamah* and the help educators. We would like to make this a communal effort and platform. Therefore, we sincerely welcome construct feedback and help in any capacity.

The goal of the *Blessed Names* series is to help children form a lasting bond with the 14 Mā'ṣūmīn by learn about and connecting with their names. We hope that you and your children enjoy these books and use them a means to achieve this goal, inshā'Allāh. We pray to Allāh to give us the strength and tawfīq to perform our duties a responsibilities.

With Duʾās,
Nabi R. Mir (Abidi)

Disclaimer: Religious texts have not been translated verbatim so as to meet the developmental and comprehens needs of children.

Kisa Kids Publications
4415 Fortran Court
San Jose, CA 95134
(260) KISA-KID [547-2543]

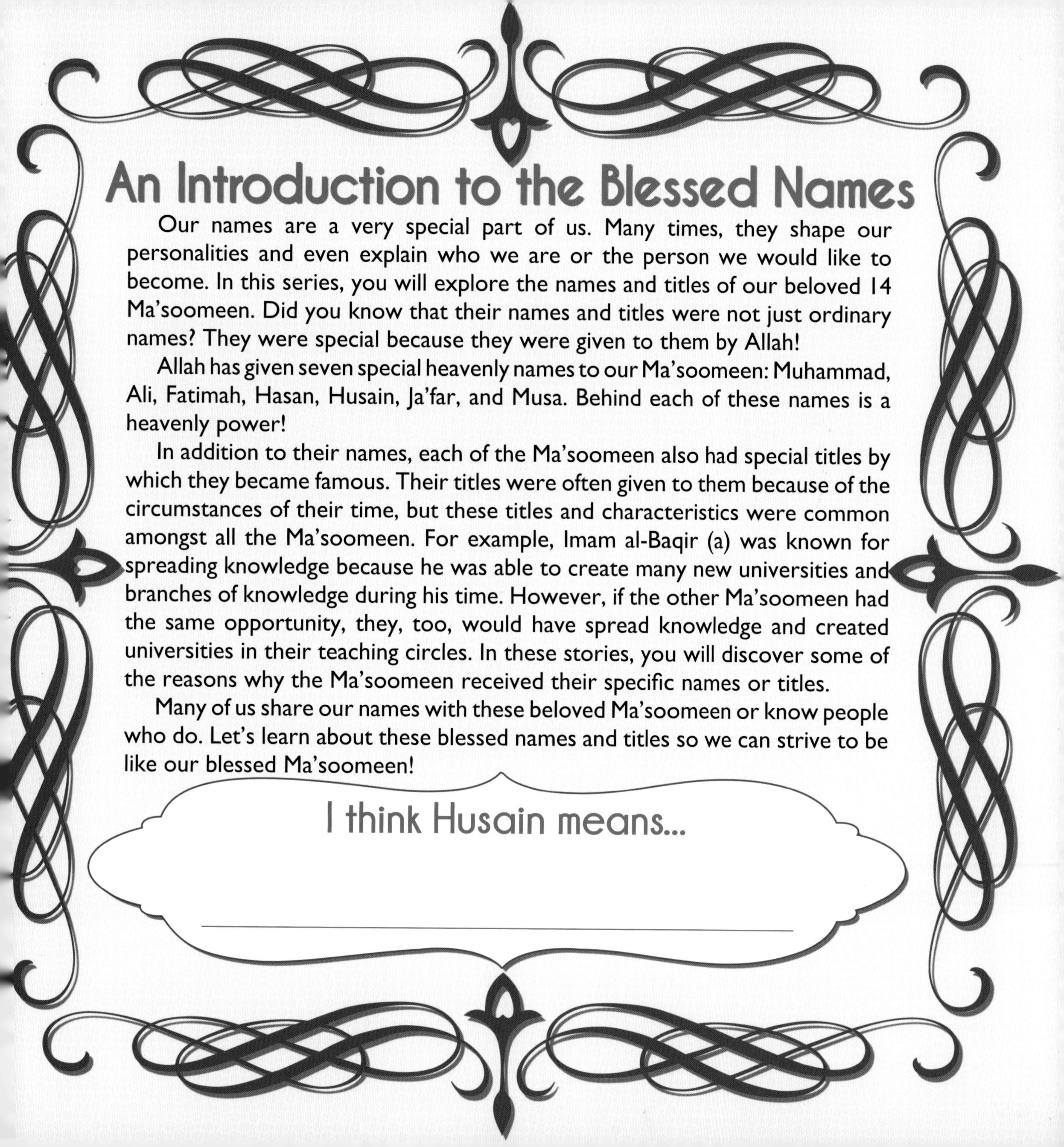

An Introduction to the Blessed Names

Our names are a very special part of us. Many times, they shape our personalities and even explain who we are or the person we would like to become. In this series, you will explore the names and titles of our beloved 14 Ma'soomeen. Did you know that their names and titles were not just ordinary names? They were special because they were given to them by Allah!

Allah has given seven special heavenly names to our Ma'soomeen: Muhammad, Ali, Fatimah, Hasan, Husain, Ja'far, and Musa. Behind each of these names is a heavenly power!

In addition to their names, each of the Ma'soomeen also had special titles by which they became famous. Their titles were often given to them because of the circumstances of their time, but these titles and characteristics were common amongst all the Ma'soomeen. For example, Imam al-Baqir (a) was known for spreading knowledge because he was able to create many new universities and branches of knowledge during his time. However, if the other Ma'soomeen had the same opportunity, they, too, would have spread knowledge and created universities in their teaching circles. In these stories, you will discover some of the reasons why the Ma'soomeen received their specific names or titles.

Many of us share our names with these beloved Ma'soomeen or know people who do. Let's learn about these blessed names and titles so we can strive to be like our blessed Ma'soomeen!

I think Husain means...

____

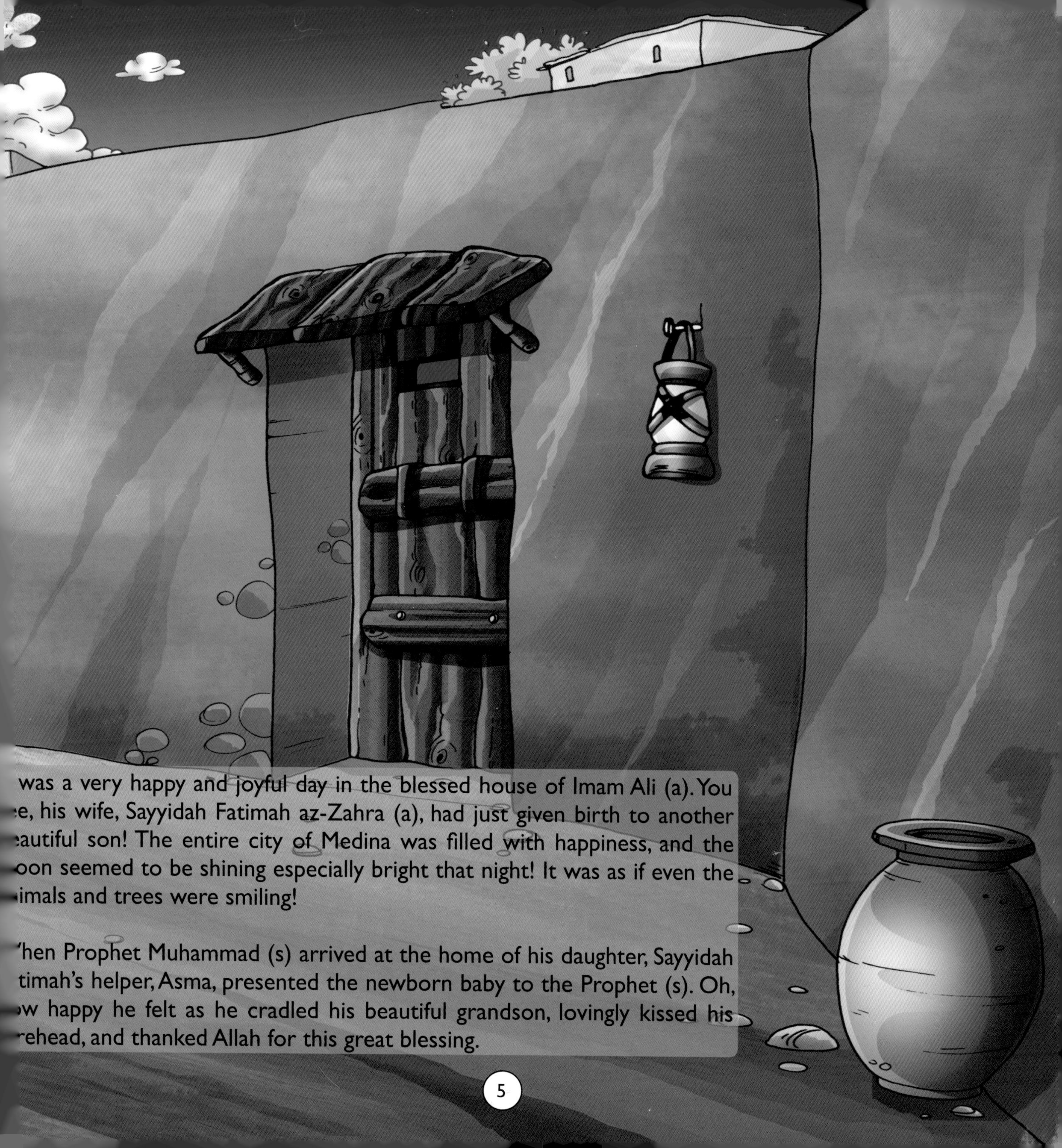

was a very happy and joyful day in the blessed house of Imam Ali (a). You
e, his wife, Sayyidah Fatimah az-Zahra (a), had just given birth to another
autiful son! The entire city of Medina was filled with happiness, and the
oon seemed to be shining especially bright that night! It was as if even the
imals and trees were smiling!

hen Prophet Muhammad (s) arrived at the home of his daughter, Sayyidah
timah's helper, Asma, presented the newborn baby to the Prophet (s). Oh,
w happy he felt as he cradled his beautiful grandson, lovingly kissed his
rehead, and thanked Allah for this great blessing.

Prophet Muhammad (s) asked Imam Ali (a), "Have you given this beautiful baby a name yet?"

Imam Ali (a) respectfully replied, "No, O Rasulullah, I could never make such an important decision without asking you first."

Prophet Muhammad (s) smiled and replied, "And I could never make such a decision without asking Allah first."

Just then, Angel Jibraeel came down from the heavens and greeted the Prophet (s). He said, "Salaamun Alaikum and congratulations on your second grandson! Allah has sent special news of a name for him. Prophet Haroon (a) was very special to his brother, Prophet Musa (a), just like Imam Ali (a) is very special to you. That is why Allah would like you to name this boy Shubair, after the youngest child of Prophet Haroon (a)." The Prophet (s) asked, "What is the Arabic name for 'Shubair?'"

Angel Jibraeel smiled and replied, "Husain."

The Prophet (s) was very happy when he heard this name. He immediately recited the Adhaan in the baby's right ear and the Iqaamah in the left ear. He then arranged for a beautiful goat to be sacrificed to feed others, especially the poor, and for Baby Husain's hair to be shaved. He was already a beautiful baby boy, but after his head was shaved, he seemed to glow brighter than the moon. The Prophet (s) then weighed his hair and gave its weight in silver as charity. Lastly, Prophet Muhammad (s) placed a small amount of perfume on Baby Husain's head and hugged him very close to his chest.

Angel Jibraeel had one more important piece of news for the Prophet (s); however, this was a sad one. Angel Jibraeel told the Prophet (s) that this sweet newborn would one day be martyred by the oppressors of his time. With a wave of his arm, he showed the Prophet (s) the exact place where Imam Husain (a) would be martyred. Upon hearing this, tears began to stream down the Prophet's face.

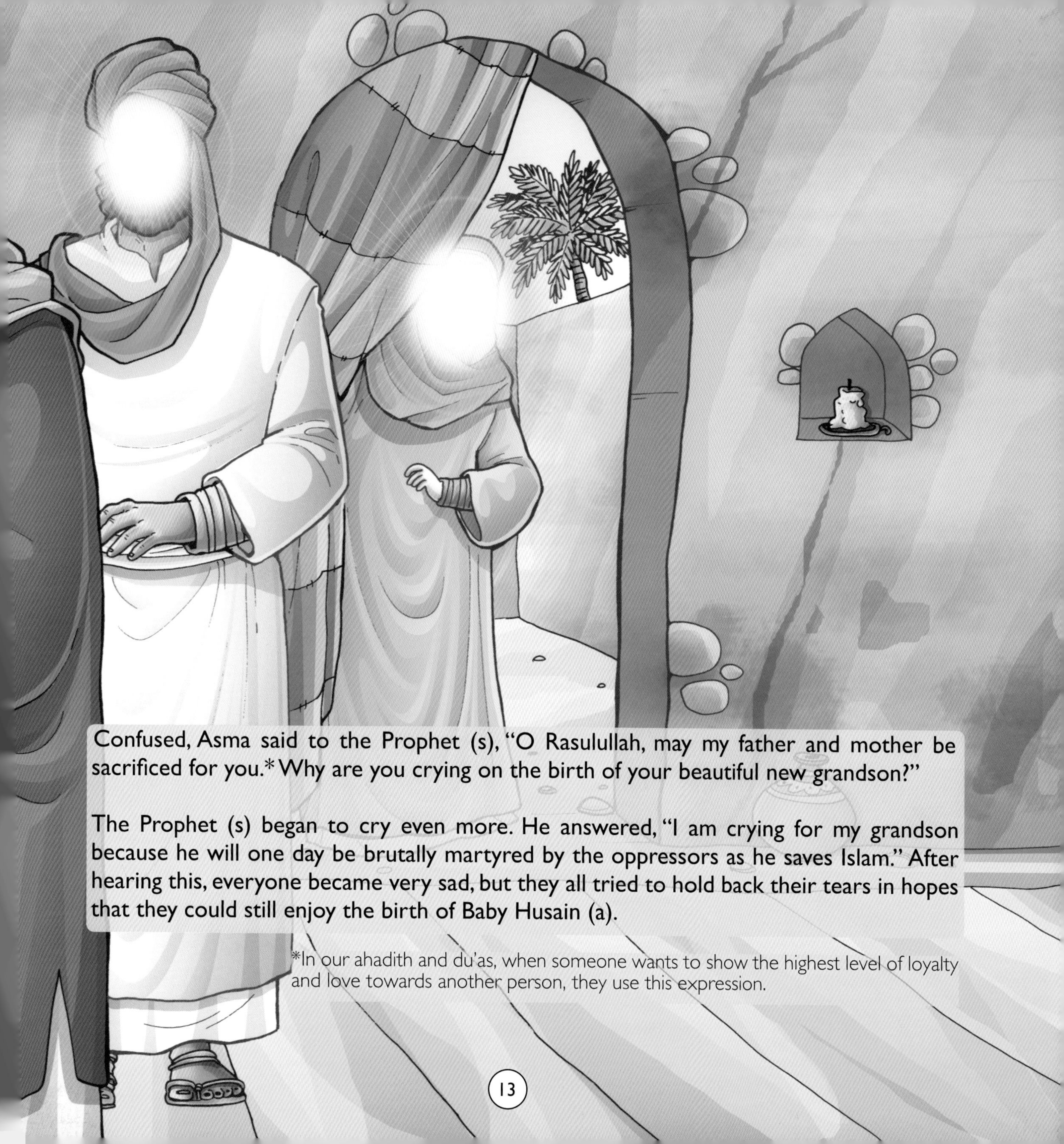

Confused, Asma said to the Prophet (s), "O Rasulullah, may my father and mother be sacrificed for you.* Why are you crying on the birth of your beautiful new grandson?"

The Prophet (s) began to cry even more. He answered, "I am crying for my grandson because he will one day be brutally martyred by the oppressors as he saves Islam." After hearing this, everyone became very sad, but they all tried to hold back their tears in hopes that they could still enjoy the birth of Baby Husain (a).

*In our ahadith and du'as, when someone wants to show the highest level of loyalty and love towards another person, they use this expression.

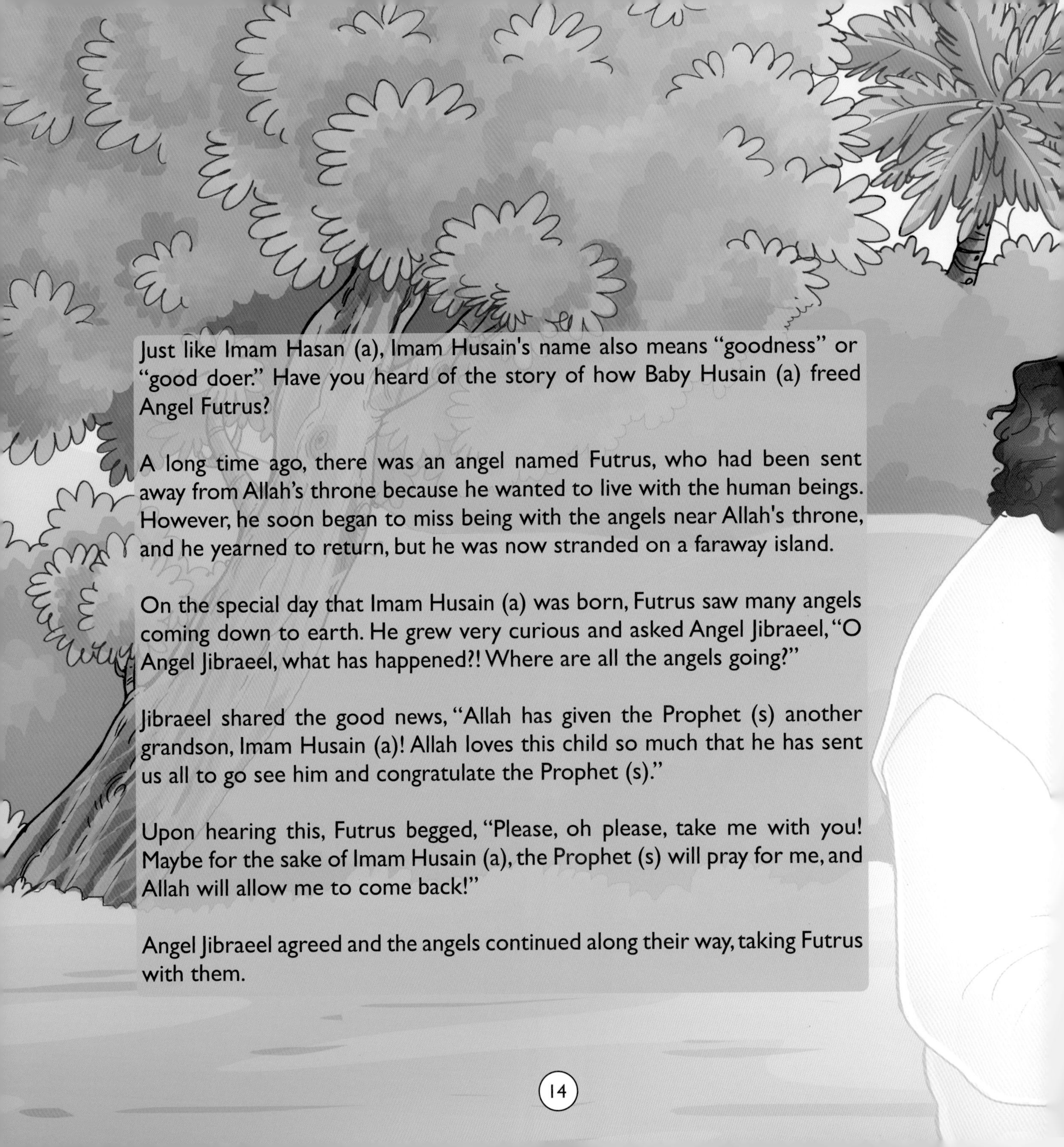

Just like Imam Hasan (a), Imam Husain's name also means "goodness" or "good doer." Have you heard of the story of how Baby Husain (a) freed Angel Futrus?

A long time ago, there was an angel named Futrus, who had been sent away from Allah's throne because he wanted to live with the human beings. However, he soon began to miss being with the angels near Allah's throne, and he yearned to return, but he was now stranded on a faraway island.

On the special day that Imam Husain (a) was born, Futrus saw many angels coming down to earth. He grew very curious and asked Angel Jibraeel, "O Angel Jibraeel, what has happened?! Where are all the angels going?"

Jibraeel shared the good news, "Allah has given the Prophet (s) another grandson, Imam Husain (a)! Allah loves this child so much that he has sent us all to go see him and congratulate the Prophet (s)."

Upon hearing this, Futrus begged, "Please, oh please, take me with you! Maybe for the sake of Imam Husain (a), the Prophet (s) will pray for me, and Allah will allow me to come back!"

Angel Jibraeel agreed and the angels continued along their way, taking Futrus with them.

As the angels entered the home of Imam Ali (a), they greeted the Prophet (s) and congratulated him on the birth of his new grandson. The Prophet (s) thanked them for their good wishes.

Angel Jibraeel then introduced Futrus to the Prophet (s) and said, "O Rasulullah, this angel left the throne of Allah and has been stranded on an island. He would like you to pray for him so that Allah may allow him to come back with us."

The Prophet (s) looked at Futrus and smiled. He said, "Rub yourself against the cradle of Baby Husain (a)."

All the other angels watched attentively as Futrus came forward and gently rubbed himself against the cradle.

MW00973540

The Castaways of the Charles Eaton

This story is based on fact. The seventeen human skulls returned to Sydney aboard the *Isabella* were first buried in the Devonshire Street Cemetery in 1904. Later, they were disinterred and reburied at Bunnering Cemetery, Botany Bay.

Thomas C. Lothian Pty Ltd
132 Albert Road, South Melbourne, Victoria 3205
www.lothian.com.au

First published 2002

National Library of Australia
Cataloguing-in-Publication data:

Crew, Gary, 1947- .
The Castaways of the Charles Eaton.

For young readers.
ISBN 0 7344 0343 7.

1. Adventure stories. 2. Shipwreck victims - Juvenile fiction.
3. Castaways - Juvenile fiction. I. Wilson, Mark. II. Title.

A823.4

Illustration media: pencil, acrylics, water colour and oil pastel
Design by John van Loon
Colour reproduction by RDC Tech Group (M) Sdn. Bhd., Malaysia
Printed in China by Leefung-Asco.

The Castaways of the Charles Eaton

Gary Crew & Mark Wilson

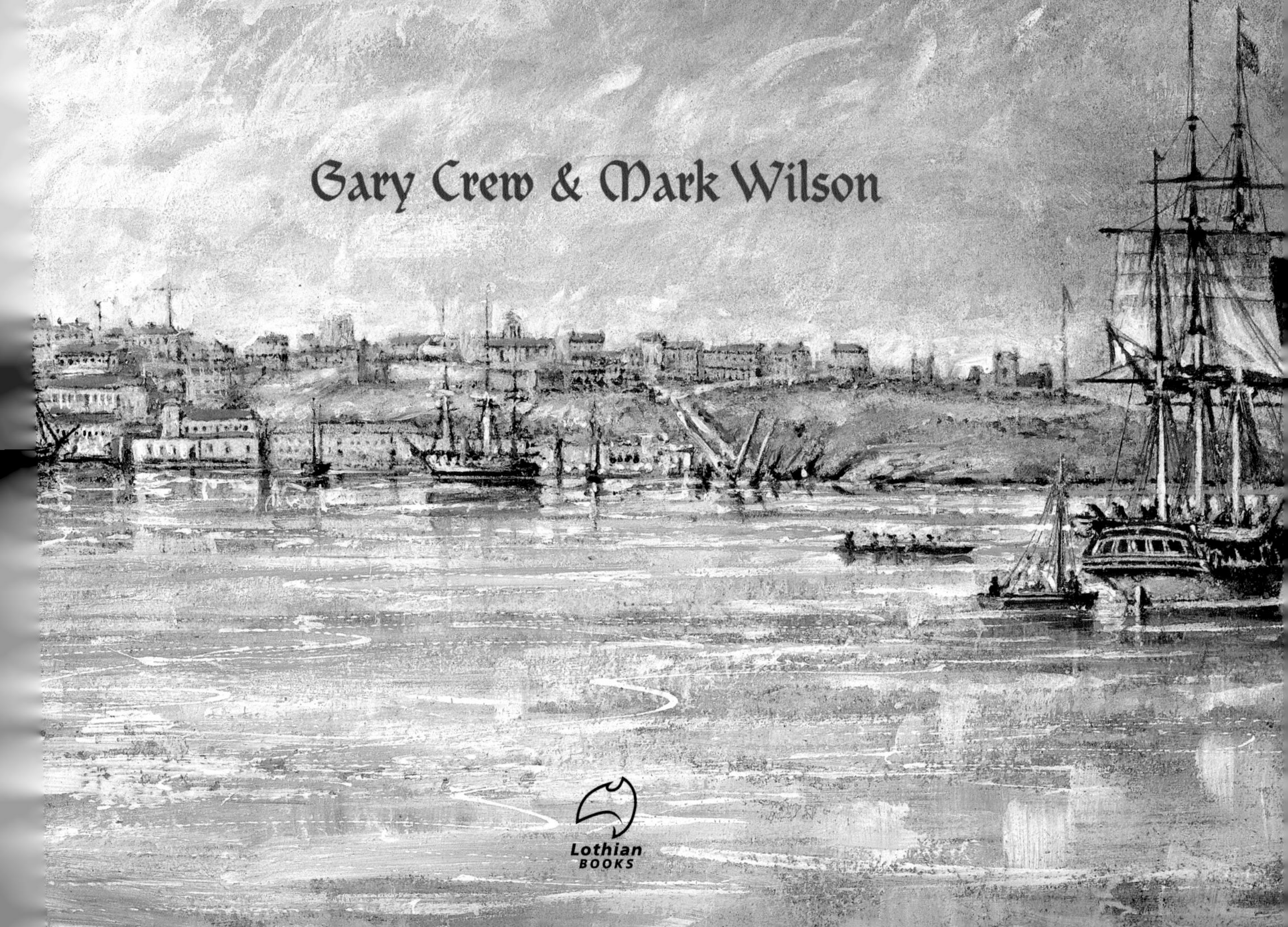

Lothian BOOKS

"On the 31st of August, 1834, the second mate and boat's
crew of the *Augustus Caesar* saw and picked up a wreck of
the S.E. side of Double Island, sufficient to convince them
that the ship *Charles Eaton* was a total wreck at some
distance to south-eastward from thence, and from the
weather they had on the 22nd, they
feared for the
safety of the crew and passengers."

THEY say that there are two sides to every story, but after what I have seen and heard, I reckon some stories could be told a hundred different ways and still not tell the truth — especially if they are sailors' yarns about castaways and head hunters.

For all of that, and hard as the task might prove, I am determined to tell you the whole story, the true and dreadful story, of the castaways of the *Charles Eaton*. And the head hunters who set upon them ...

YOU see, it was me, Midshipman Walter Lewellyn, fifteen years old and ship's clerk of the schooner *Isabella*, who Captain Lewis ordered to talk to the castaways after we had rescued them.

So I came to know Jack Ireland, cabin boy of the *Charles Eaton* and little William D'Oyley, miserable castaway creatures that they were.

'Keep those boys calm, Mr Lewellyn,' the Captain ordered. 'And you might try to teach 'em proper English while you're at it. They've been with those head-hunting cannibals more than two years now, talking their Babel tongue. Besides, that little one was no more than a baby when they took his father's head off. And his mother's too. God rest her soul.'

THE *Isabella* sailed from Sydney on the 3rd of June, 1836, under the command of Captain Charles Lewis. Our orders were to search for survivors of the *Charles Eaton*, a vessel believed to have foundered on the Great Barrier Reef in August, 1834.

Twenty-six passengers and crew were aboard, mostly members of the Bengal Artillery returning to India under the command of Captain D'Oyley, along with his wife, Charlotte, and two of their three sons, George, aged seven, and William, aged two.

THE boys' Indian 'ayah', or nurse, was also with them and if Jack Ireland's version of what happened is true, she had her head cut off too — but I will say no more of that at the moment. It is better that I do not hurry, and tell this story right.

The truth is that the *Isabella* was only sent to look for the wreck of the *Charles Eaton* because two years before, Captain Carr of the British ship, *Mangles*, reported that he had seen a white boy aboard a native proa in the vicinity of the Murray Islands.

Try as I might, I have not been able to discover what Captain Carr was doing in those waters. In fact, his being there was decidedly odd. The islands thereabouts were known to be crawling with head hunters.

What's more, while white sailors will never admit to trading in human heads, I have seen such heads in England. Mounted, they are, and put in glass cases, and shown to the public for a penny.

Whether Captain Carr was trading for heads or otherwise, certain important people in England read his report about seeing a white boy and grew very concerned. And so, on the off chance that the boy might be one of the D'Oyley children who had been aboard the long-lost *Charles Eaton*, the *Isabella* was commissioned to discover the truth.

UPON reaching Murray Island, the *Isabella* was at once surrounded by four huge canoes. Each was filled with islanders, calling, 'Poued! Poued!'. I now know that this word means 'Peace', although by the look of the natives' painted faces I would not have believed so at the time.

In the hope that the mysterious white boy might still be in the area, and not wanting to stir up the natives, Captain Lewis ordered our guns to be run in so that they might not be seen. Then he told the crew to show the axes we had brought for trade.

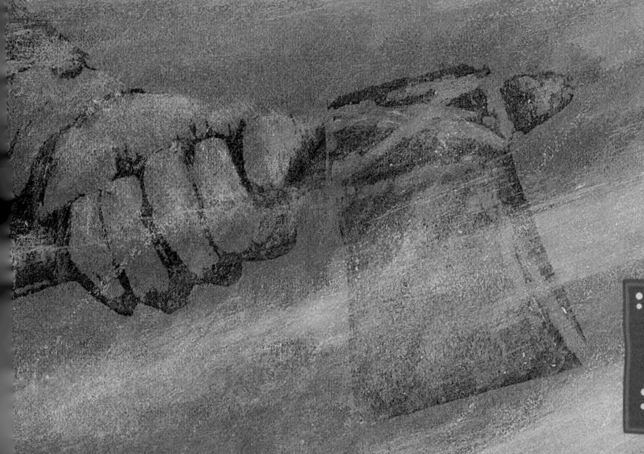

HE Captain made signs that the natives could have what they wanted if they gave us the white boy, which was strange considering he was far from certain that such a boy was there. Still, he called me on deck and ordered that I strip naked. When I did [unhappily, I admit] he pointed at me and then at the island. By such means the natives understood that he was looking for a white boy — but the bribes he offered were not enough to tempt them to help. Seeing this, the Captain ordered me below, shouting, 'No white skin, no axes!' After some heated parley, the natives returned to the shore to disappear among the coco-a-nut palms.

The Captain continued to sweep the island with his glass, and within the hour his hope was rewarded. A single proa cast off. Even with the naked eye I could make out a pale skinned boy squatting amidships.

'They have him!' the Captain cried and immediately ordered that ropes be lowered. But when the proa drew alongside, we were amazed to see the boy was loathe to leave his native companions.

'Mr Lewellyn,' the captain called, 'this boy appears to be about your age. You may have more hope of convincing him to join us.'

I leant over the gunwale and saw the boy directly below. Apart from our age, we had little in common. At least, I hoped that was so. I prided myself on the cleanliness of my appearance, but this boy's hair was long and tangled and he wore no more than a soiled and ragged loin cloth.

NEVERTHELESS, I did as the Captain ordered and called, 'My name is Lewellyn. This is the *Isabella*, an English vessel, come to rescue you. Take a rope and climb aboard. Have no fear. We are all Englishmen and His Majesty's loyal subjects.'

I know that the boy heard me but he turned away, seeking comfort in the arms of an old savage who held him close and eyed us fearfully.

'What ship are you from?' I continued.

Though he still clung to the old man, to my amazement he muttered, 'Chareetie.' And again, 'Chareetie.'

'Ah!' I heard the Captain breathe beside me. 'The *Charles Eaton* ...'

'What is your name?' I persisted, gathering courage.

The boy touched his chest. 'Wak,' he answered, and then, holding the old man, 'Duppa. Duppa.'

'You! Duppa!' the Captain called. 'You want axe? You give me boy. Give me Wak ...'

Duppa shook his head.

'Two axes?' my master asked, holding them up. At three the old man stood unsteadily then hauled the boy up beside him. When the axes had been handed down, he took hold of a rope and clambered aboard, pushing the unwilling boy from behind.

WHILE Duppa was given more gifts, the Captain had me fetch the official record of those who had been aboard the *Charles Eaton*. I sat on the deck and read the name of each person aloud. From time to time the boy nodded, seeming to remember someone, but when I read the name, 'Jack Ireland, cabin boy,' he fairly whooped with joy.

'Me,' he cried. 'Me, Wak. Me, Jack Ireland!'

At last we had made some headway. And when I read the name, 'William D'Oyley,' he pointed a grubby finger at the page and laughed. 'He here. He alive. He name Uass.'

'Alive?' the captain repeated. 'What? The younger one?' Then turning to me, he whispered, 'This is good for us. The D'Oyleys are important people. Wealthy. With influence. This is very good indeed.'

I failed to understand why a boy from a wealthy family should be thought of as more important than any other, but I said nothing.

'And where is this boy?' the Captain demanded.

'Uass little. He on island. Oby his fadder now. Oby love him.'

'Can you help us save him too?'

Jack Ireland looked hard at the Captain then at Duppa who, having heard the names Uass and Oby, now gave us his attention.

'There are no more left alive?' I asked.

Jack turned towards the island. For a long time he remained silent, possibly remembering, then he sighed. 'No,' he said. 'No.'

THAT night Jack and Duppa shared a pallet on the deck under the eye of the sailor on watch. I could not sleep and sat close by. But come dawn, when Duppa made signs that he would return to land, Jack clung to him, begging him to remain. Duppa would not.

So we waited until mid-morning when a crowd of islanders appeared on the shore. From a distance we could not read their intention until, raising his glass, the Captain shouted, 'There is a white child with them.'

'Willam D'Oyley?' I asked.

'No,' Jack Ireland said. 'He no William. He Uass now, son of Oby.'

I admit that the child seemed so happy playing with the other children on the beach I wished we could have weighed anchor and left him there, but the Captain had the crew drape yards of tempting sailcloth over the side and flash the bright axes in the sun.

In no time a proa pulled alongside and there was the child staring up. Duppa was with him and another old man, who I took to be Oby. Like Duppa before him, he could not resist the axes, and though the little boy wept, he was soon hoisted aboard.

'Get them below,' the Captain ordered. 'Keep them calm ...'

I took William in my arms and motioned for Jack to follow, but once below decks the little one began to scream and bite. No soft words would settle him. Finally I opened my sea chest and took out a box of toy soldiers which had travelled with me since I was a child. To my surprise the boy fell quiet at once, parading the soldiers about as if he had observed the changing of the guard every day of his life. I thought him a proper little Englishman!

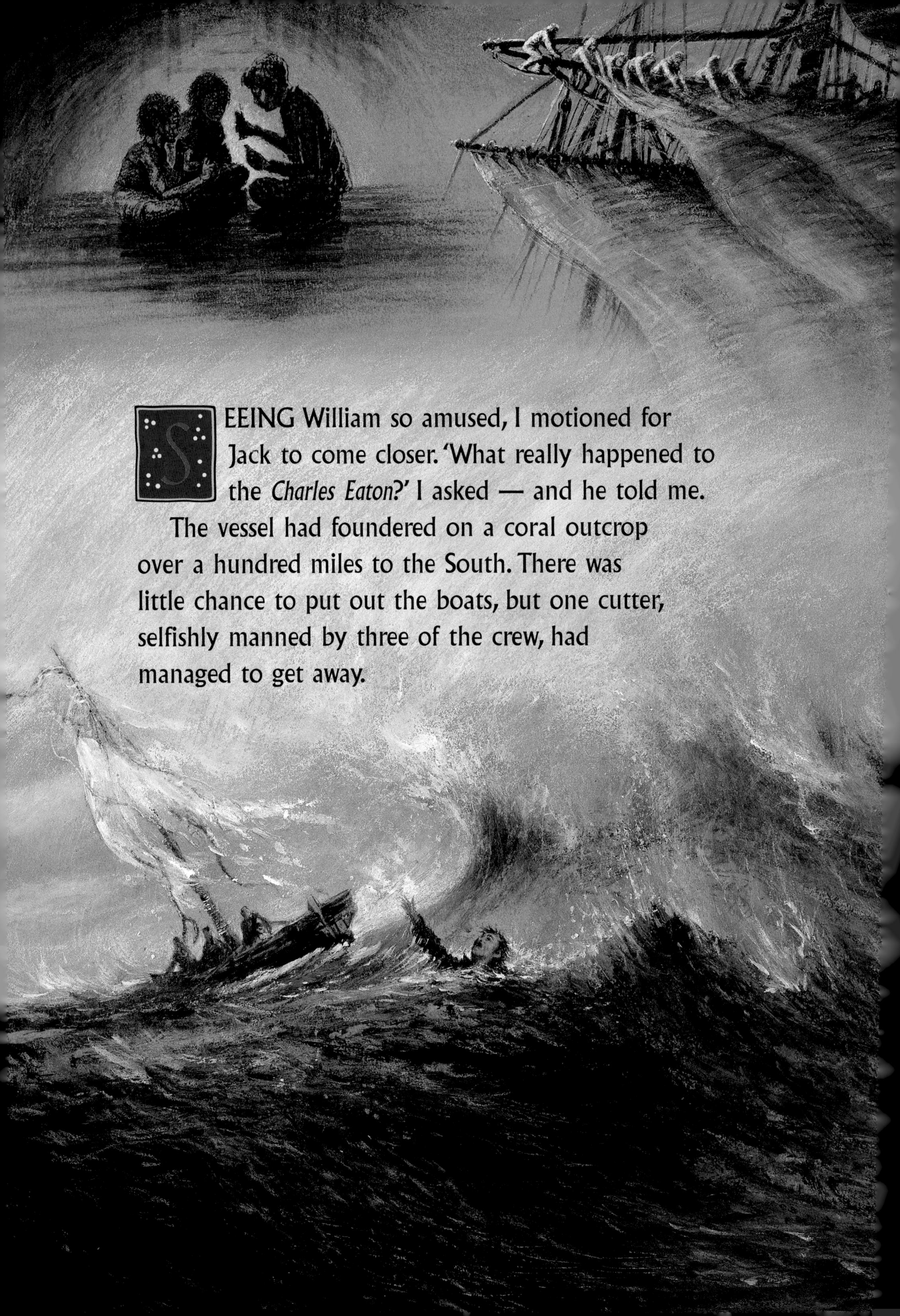

SEEING William so amused, I motioned for Jack to come closer. 'What really happened to the *Charles Eaton*?' I asked — and he told me.

The vessel had foundered on a coral outcrop over a hundred miles to the South. There was little chance to put out the boats, but one cutter, selfishly manned by three of the crew, had managed to get away.

CHARLES EATON

LEFT with little hope, those who remained aboard built a raft. Upon it Captain Lewis put the 'important people' — the D'Oyleys and their children, George and little William — and a few seamen to assist them, but not Jack nor the other cabin boy, Sexton. The raft rode out the night tied to the sinking *Charles Eaton* but in the morning those who remained on deck found that it had been cut adrift, leaving them to their fate.

So much for 'important people'!

Those unfortunates who had been left behind built yet another raft. After drifting for two days, they were found by Islanders [claiming to be friendly] and towed ashore.

Only then did Jack Ireland notice that the first raft had been dragged onto the same beach — a circumstance which struck him as more than a coincidence. But this realisation came too late. The murders had begun ...

Wanting heads, the natives set about killing the crew the moment they came ashore. Captain D'Oyley and his wife were beheaded in front of their children, William D'Oyley being torn screaming from his mother's arms. Nor did the horror cease until the waves broke red with blood.

BUT, strange to say, the boys were spared. The D'Oyleys because they were so young, and Jack and Sexton because they fought back. You see, the islanders believed that these boys were 'laamars', or the ghosts of their own dead children returned with white skins. So Jack was taken by Duppa, and William by Oby.

'Who took George D'Oyley and Sexton?' I asked. 'And where are they?'

'Gone,' was all Jack said. 'Gone.'

'Gone where?'

'They die.'

'What? They were murdered too?'

Jack shook his head. 'No. Duppa says they dead because they kept in.'

'Kept in what?'

'In haus. Inwards. No sun.'

'In a house? A hut? And never allowed out?'

'Yes. They fadder think they run away. Get taken by bad spirit. They die inside haus. Bad. Bad …' At this he rubbed his face and arms.

'Their skin went bad? Is that what you are saying?'

'Skin, yes. Bawls.'

'Boils?'

'Bawls. Bad,' he nodded and turning, he pulled down the breeches we had given him. I saw that his backside was scarred all over. He had been afflicted himself.

'So they are both dead?' I asked, motioning for him to dress.

'Yes, dead,' he whispered, lowering his eyes. 'But here, with us.'

'No,' I corrected him. 'They are in Heaven. In the arms of Jesus.'

'No, no, no!' he laughed. 'I take you all to see. Them dead, yes, but their spirit still here. I show you …'

TRUE to his word, the next day Jack helped navigate the *Isabella* to Aureed Island. Once ashore, he lost no time in directing our party to a native hut. 'These the dead from the Chareetie,' Jack said, pointing. 'You see? The spirit still there!'

Mounted on the walls we saw a great shield made of tortoiseshell. It was surrounded with human skulls. The thing was so horrible I almost disgraced myself but Captain Lewis was made of sterner stuff. 'Seventeen skulls,' he said, his tone matter of fact. 'All that is left of the company of the *Charles Eaton*. I am certain ...'

WHEN I had settled myself, I looked at the skulls more carefully. One still had a long, blonde plait attached. If this was Mrs D'Oyley, where was the other woman, the ayah? Search as I might, I could see no sign of her and set to wondering if she held no special charm for the head-hunters. Being dark, had she looked too much like themselves?

It seemed that this woman had not mattered to anybody. All that the Charles Eaton's passenger list had to say about her was: 'One Native. India. Servant'. Neither had the blacks mounted her skull. So she had no memorial, not so much as a name.

Though Jack Ireland was able to name the actual murderers — who had not even come from Aureed — it seemed that all black men were the same to Captain Lewis.

Enraged at what he had seen, the Captain destroyed every native hut he could find, the surrounding coco-a-nut trees, every proa and every fishing net. Then he burned the island to the ground.

The next day the *Isabella* sailed away: the shield and skulls in her hold, the castaway boys in my cabin.

When we reached Sydney, Jack Ireland stayed with me at The Sailor's Inn. He seemed happy enough — but one night, without a word, he slipped away.

I never saw him again.

The fate of young William D'Oyley proved quite a different matter. Being the orphaned son of an important family, he was personally escorted to London by Captain Lewis himself — taking my toy soldiers with him. So much for important people.

But I care very little. Apart from the words that I have written, which are as close as I can come to the truth, what need have I for reminders of the past?

None, if the truth is told.

No, not so much as a human skull ...

WITHIN THIS TOMB WERE INTERRED ON XXVI NOVEMBER, MDCCXXXVI,
THE REMAINS OF SEVENTEEN HUMAN BODIES.
DISCOVERED, AFTER THE MOST DILIGENT RESEARCH, IN THE ISLAND OF AUREED IN TORRES STRAIT,
BY C.M. LEWIS, COMMANDER OF H.M. COLONIAL SCHOONER "ISABELLA" AND BY SATISFACTORY
EVIDENCE IDENTIFIED AS THE MORTAL REMAINS OF CERTAIN OF THE OFFICERS, CREW AND PASSENGERS
OF THE BARK "CHARLES EATON", WHO, AFTER ESCAPING FROM THE TOTAL WRECK OF THAT VESSEL,
ON XV AUGUST, MDCCCXXXIV, WERE SAVAGELY MASSACRED BY THE NATIVES ON THE ISLANDS ON WHICH
THEY LANDED.
HIS EXCELLENCY SIR RICHARD BOURKE, K.C.B. GOVERNOR IN CHIEF OF THIS COLONY, BY WHOSE
COMMAND THE EXPEDITION TO ASCERTAIN THE FATE OF THESE UNHAPPY PERSONS WAS UNDERTAKEN,
CAUSED THE LAST OFFICES OF PIETY TO BE DISCHARGED TOWARDS THEM, BY DIRECTING THE
INTERMENT OF THEIR REMAINS WITH THE RITES OF CHRISTIAN BURIAL, AND THE ERECTION OF THIS
MONUMENT TO RECORD THE CATASTROPHE BY WHICH THEY PERISHED.
"AND THEY TOLD DAVID, SAYING, THAT THE MEN OF JABESH-GILEAD WERE THEY THAT BURIED
SAUL". AND DAVID SENT MESSENGERS "TO THE MEN OF JABESH-GILEAD AND SAID UNTO THEM
BLESSED BE YE OF THE LORD, THAT YE HAVE SHOWN THIS KINDNESS".
11.SAM.11 - IV.V.

NEU HOLLA